# An Insider's Guide to Ace

# System

# Design

## Interviews

A Quick Guide to Answer System Design Interview
Questions

**MAURICE**

# JAYSON

# Copyright

# Table of Contents

# CHAPTER ONE

## INTRODUCTION TO SYSTEM DESIGN INTERVIEW QUESTIONS

---

Systems design interviews are becoming a standard part of the hiring process. The effectiveness in system design interviews reflects your ability to work with complex systems. Solving system design interview questions can get you into your desired job position with a high salary and other companies' incentives.

Most engineers fear System Design Interviews (SDIs) partly because of their lack of experience designing large scalable systems and partly because of the unstructured nature of SDIs. Even engineers who are experienced in building such systems are not very comfortable with these interviews. The main reason for this is that the systems design interview does not have standard answers and is open-ended.

# WHAT IS SYSTEM DESIGN?

System design is a set of rules and tools for visual and technical execution that reflects a product's philosophy and is constantly evolving. This definition may not be clear now, but it will become clearer as we progress in this e-book.

# SCALING FROM ZERO TO MILLIONS OF USERS

The systems design phenomenon has gained popularity over the last decades, and it is no surprise to job seekers anymore to come across questions of sort. When the system design interview started, those who partook in such an interview had nothing to focus on. But in this e-book, I will show you how to answer most questions from the interviewer.

# FIVE GUIDELINES FOR SYSTEM DESIGN INTERVIEWS

1. If you are faced with a system design question, you don't need to panic or hurry.

2. You don't need to reveal or explain in many details; just provide the pivotal point.

3. Ignore unnecessary necessities and set your mind on the architectural aspect.

4. In the system interview, you must keep it simple and clear.

5. Most people fail system design questions because they forget to look at the big picture.

6. Avoid too many hacks when solving any mathematical complication.

7. Endeavor to justify any points highlighted in your defense. Don't use buzz words or incomplete knowledge in your design.

8. Before attempting any question, be aware of the recent outcomes and technological practices.

**NOTE:** System design interviews are not that difficult to answer if you have accustomed yourself with the requested knowledge from books like this. Lastly, you should be able to argue for a custom implementation with its pros and cons.

## POINT OF EVALUATION FROM SYSTEM DESIGN INTERVIEW

### 1. The clarity of answer or thought

Interviewers want to see how you can express your thoughts correctly and confidently. You should also be able to justify any decision you are taking. This is because, in the system design interview, there is enough room to argue your point and clear doubts. If your interviewer asks you a difficult question, you must use standard approaches to tackle it. For instance, let's say the interviewer asked you to create APIs. It would be best if you start by stating some replication, as this will help increase availability in general. It is quite easy to present the solution to the answer. NOTE: As I said earlier, never state any points without understanding the concept properly. You are likely going to get half or no mark for half answer.

## 2. Level of Knowledge and Terminology

Your level of knowledge is seen in using the right terminology. Therefore, you have to be abreast of relevant and current facts in the market. This comes with attempting several products and design practices.

You should know when to point out the solution clearly and when to build custom around it. After you have named a product, for example, endeavor to give the product's relevant feature. Design practices allow you to confront certain custom requirements. Examples of such are decoupling systems, load balancing, sticky sessions, etc.

## 3. Your Flexibility and Response

You should be able to quickly shift your from one domain to another without confusing your interviewer. This is because your interviewer is interested in your level of expertise, i.e., how well you know about the system's different parts.

It is wise not to have a particular architecture in mind. In the System design interview, we all try to fit requirements to a system, but only after the initial ones have shaped it. A rigid or sentimental behavior builds a brittle architecture that will likely not work properly or fail.

Before procuring any answer, think about the question clearly and understand it properly to the smallest unit. Afterward, focus on a specific aspect to start from and proceed to the next. Just endeavor to take it one step at a time. Certain areas can be extracted out and explained properly to clarify doubt in the system.

# CHAPTER TWO

## UNMASKING THE SECRET BEHIND SYSTEM DESIGN INTERVIEW

---

### WHAT IS A SYSTEM DESIGN INTERVIEW?

For newbies on this topic, I will briefly explain. For most top companies such as Google, Facebook, and Uber, at least one of the on-site interviews is a system design interview.

In this interview, you will be asked to design a specific system and have a heated discussion on all the details with the interviewer. However, since this question is quite open, the interviewer can decide the direction of the discussion. With this in mind, even for the same question, you may have completely different discussions with different interviewers.

This is why I never worry about whether the interviewer has ever seen this problem. Let's take the problem of "designing a web crawler" as an example.

As an interviewer, I can focus the interview on the entire crawler infrastructure. I can specifically discuss how to remove URLs. I can also ask how to detect whether the page has been updated. You may also be asked to write some code in the system design interview. But I don't see much difference from the general programming interview.

## HOW TO EVALUATE THE SYSTEM DESIGN INTERVIEW.

I firmly believe that if you can't evaluate a thing, you can't improve it. Most people don't know how to evaluate the system design interview; how do they prepare? It's like you are playing a game without knowing the rules.

Unlike programming interviews, there are no standard answers to system design questions, so the evaluation process is more subjective. However, as an interviewer, I still have something.

First, I will assess whether the design is effective. Although there is no implementation to verify, based on work experience and some common sense, if this question is given, I will ask myself if I will try the proposed method. In most cases, it is obvious to judge whether there is a problem with the design. I just use some examples to challenge the candidates. For example, if I ask him to check whether a certain URL has been crawled before, I will see if the solution handles such short URLs or URLs with UTM parameters. This is the minimum requirement. If the candidate can't do this, I won't go into it, or I may ask another question.

Secondly, I will check the feasibility. Some candidates will propose solutions that are only effective in theory. It may require unlimited memory or the system is not very complicated. In any case, I will ask him to solve this problem. A good way to verify it is to ask yourself how much time and how many engineers it will implement the design. I prefer a relaxed and simple design. If you can't make a prototype within a week or two, I might ask you to simplify it.

Sometimes, most candidates will develop a complex solution requiring much data and some ML components and pipelines. It is difficult to achieve in reality because it is very risky. You don't want to spend a year on this unproven idea; it may just not work.

Third, I hope the candidate knows what he is talking about. More specifically, I want to make sure he knows why the system should be designed specifically, the constraints, and other solutions. Often, design issues are vaguely described. A good candidate can tell you what the hypothesis is and how to compare the design with others. To make it clearer, ask yourself an alternative solution and why the system was built in this way instead of other solutions.

In the following sections, we will focus on some practical tips and use them to get started.

# HOW TO PREPARE FOR SYSTEM DESIGN INTERVIEW

We have to admit that experience trumps everything. This is why some experienced engineers do not need preparation at all. However, there are many things you can do to make major changes.

**Project**

If you are still some time away from your interview (at least six months), building something is worth it. Everyone can participate in the macro design, but only those who work on the details can consider everything.

If you are a student, you can take an internship, and you can also work on projects that interest you. It is also a good idea to contribute to some open-source projects. The important thing is not which project to work on, but something to work on.

This is very important because you don't know whether your design is effective without actual work. With some practical experience, you will quickly realize that many things are difficult to achieve, but at first glance, they seem reasonable. For example, if you want to check whether the web page's content has been updated since the last crawl and rely on whether the HTML remains the same, you will find that many web pages have the same content, but the comments, sidebars, etc. have been changed. This is a design that I think is not applicable, although it sounds reasonable.

## Curiosity

It is usually very important to be curious about everything. A good practice is to choose any product you use every day, such as YouTube, and think about how you will design the system from scratch.

Sometimes the product may be very complicated; you can also design a feature like Facebook friend recommendation. If you have time, writing some code to implement a prototype is a plus. But the important thing is that you should try to go into the details.

Although there are no standard answers to system design questions, you can still search for implementing these products/functions. Compare it with your design to understand the difference. High Scalability is highly recommended, but don't spend too much time on specific tools.

Note: A trick is that many interviewers like to ask company-related design questions. For example, you are more likely to design Google products/features in a Google interview. This is not always the case, but the company's products or similar products should be valued.

**Practice**

Similar to coding problems, you also need to practice system design interviews. There are several ways. You can do some Google searches to see how others will deal with the same problem and compare it with your design. For example, the system design interview question set is a very detailed analysis of common problems. A better way is to practice with more experienced people. If you have friends who have been in the industry for a while, that would be great. Ask them for help. I think interactive exercises are always better because the whole interview process is more like a discussion than exams.

## What is not important?

A common mistake is that many people place too much emphasis on specific technologies. For example, they spent a lot of time using AWS, configuring the Google cloud platform, and using a specific web framework. I'm not saying these are useless, but they are good things. However, from the perspective of system design interviews, I think interviewers are more concerned with understanding knowledge than specific techniques.

For example, when discussing big processing data, as an interviewer, I want to discuss how to distribute data to multiple machines, aggregate them together, and distribute the load evenly. If someone tells me he will use Hadoop on AWS, I will ask for more details, and he will eventually answer all the questions above. The thumb rule focuses more on how each tool is designed, rather than what tools to use.

## CONCLUSION

All the tips for the system design interview are difficult to complete in one chapter. We will discuss some live strategies in the next chapter.

# CHAPTER THREE

## MORE UNDERSTANDING ON API

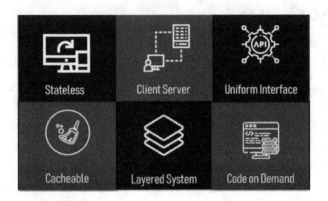

## What is an API?

An API is a set of protocols that facilitate the creation and integration of application software. API is an acronym that stands for "Application Programming Interface."

## What are APIs used for?

APIs allow your product or service to communicate with other products and services without knowing their implementation details. They simplify application development, saving you time and money. When you design new tools and products or manage existing ones, APIs give you more flexibility, simplify design, administration, use, and empower you to innovate.

APIs are sometimes seen as contracts, with documentation that constitutes an agreement between the parties. If part 1 sends a remote request according to a particular structure, the software in part 2 will respond according to the defined conditions.

## Why are APIs important?

Because APIs simplify the way developers integrate new application components into existing architecture, they facilitate collaboration between IT and business teams. Often, business needs to change rapidly in the face of ever-changing digital markets, where new competitors can turn an entire industry upside down with a new application.

To maintain their competitiveness, these companies need to support the rapid development and deployment of innovative services. Developing cloud-native applications is an obvious way to increase development speed. It is based on the connection of a micro services type application architecture via APIs.

APIs are a simplified way to connect your infrastructure through cloud-native application development. They also allow you to share your data with your customers and other external users. Public APIs offer unique business value because they can simplify and grow your relationships with your partners, and potentially monetize your data (the Google Maps API is a perfect example).

## Concrete API examples

Imagine a book distributor. This distributor could provide its client bookstores with an application that allows them to check the availability of books with the supplier. But the development of this application may be expensive and take a long time, while the final application may be limited by the platform and require continuous maintenance.

The distributor can also provide an API to check stock availability. This approach has several advantages. By accessing data through an API, customers can centralize information about their inventory. The distributor can modify its internal systems without impacting its customers' experience, as long as its API's behavior does not change. With a public API, developers who work for the distributor, bookstores, or other businesses can develop an application that helps customers find the books they want to buy. Thus, distributors can increase their sales or seize new business opportunities.

## Are APIs secure?

APIs allow you to open up access to your resources without sacrificing control and security. You choose which resources you want to share and with whom. The security of APIs depends, above all, on their good management. Connecting APIs and building applications that use the data or functionality exposed by APIs can be done through a distributed integration platform that connects everything, including legacy systems and the Internet of Things.

There are three approaches to accessing APIs;

**1. Private APIs**

The API can only be used internally. This approach allows you to keep full control over the API.

**2. Partner APIs**

The API is shared with some business partners. This approach can generate new revenue streams without compromising security.

**3. Public APIs**

The API is accessible to everyone. This approach allows third parties to develop applications that interact with your API and become a source of innovation.

## How APIs Drive Innovation

By making your APIs accessible to your partners as well as to third parties, you can:

1. Generate new revenue channels or expand existing ones

2. Extend the reach of your brand

3. Stimulate open source innovation or improve efficiency through external development and collaboration.

**What is the role of APIs in all of this?**

Imagine a business partner developing an app that allows customers to locate the books they are looking for on the shelves. By improving the customer experience, this application will attract other customers to the bookstore, itself a customer of the distributor, who will ultimately have extended its revenue channel.

A third-party company can also use a public API to develop an application so that customers can purchase books directly from the distributor, without going through the bookstore. In this case, the distributor will have opened a new revenue channel.

A business can benefit from sharing its APIs with some of its partners or with the world. Each partnership allows you to expand your brand awareness alongside your marketing campaigns. By making your technologies public, with a public API, you encourage developers to create an ecosystem of applications around your API. The more people use your technology, the more likely they are to do business with you.

You can thus obtain results that are as unexpected as they are interesting by opening up access to your technologies, and these results can sometimes upset an entire sector. In our book distributor, new businesses, such as a book rental service, can cause a fundamental change in how it operates. Public and partner APIs let you take advantage of innovations from a larger developer community. Innovative ideas can sprout anywhere. Businesses need to stay abreast of changes in their marketplace and prepare for them. This is where APIs come in.

## APIs History

APIs appeared at the dawn of computing, even before personal computers. At that time, they were mostly used as libraries for operating systems. Almost all of them resided locally on the systems they ran on, although they occasionally transferred messages between mainframes. Almost 30 years later, APIs have left their local environments. In the early 2000s, they became important for remote data integration.

## Remote APIs

Remote APIs are designed to interact with a communications network. Here, "remote" means that the API's resources are not located on the computer that formulates the request. As the most frequently used communication network is the Internet, most APIs are designed based on web standards. Not all remote APIs are web APIs, but it can be assumed that all web APIs are remote.

Web APIs typically use the HTTP protocol for their request messages and define the structure of response messages. Most of the time, response messages are in the form of an XML or JSON file. These two formats are the most common because their data is easy to manipulate for other applications.

## API improvements

APIs have continued to grow in the now ubiquitous web, and several initiatives have attempted to simplify their design and increase their usefulness.

## SOAP and REST

Simpler than SOAP   Documentation   Error messages

To standardize information exchange between the increasingly numerous APIs, it was necessary to develop a protocol: the "Simple Object Access

Protocol" or SOAP. APIs designed after the SOAP protocol use XML format for their messages and receive requests via HTTP or SMTP.

SOAP aims to simplify information exchange between applications that run in different environments or are written in different languages. Representational State Transfer, or REST, is another attempt at standardization. Web APIs that respect the constraints of the REST architecture are called RESTful APIs.

These two elements differ on one fundamental point: SOAP is a protocol, while REST is an architecture style. This means that there is no official standard that governs REST web APIs. According to the definition proposed by Roy Fielding in his thesis "Architectural Styles and the Design of Network-based Software Architectures," APIs are RESTful as long as they respect the six design constraints of a RESTful system.

A client-server architecture: a REST architecture comprises clients, servers, and resources, and it processes requests via the HTTP protocol.

**A stateless server:** Client content is never stored on the server between requests. Information about the session state is stored on the client.

**Cache memory:** caching eliminates the need for certain interactions between the client and the server.

**A layered system:** additional layers can mediate interactions between client and server. These layers can perform additional functions, such as load balancing, cache sharing, or security.

**Code on demand:** A server can extend a client's functionality by transferring executable code to it.

**Uniform interface:** This constraint is essential for the design of RESTful APIs and covers four different aspects:

**Identification of resources in requests:** Resources are identified in requests and are separated from represent-tations returned to the client.

**Manipulation of resources by representations:** Clients receive files that represent the resources. These representations must contain enough information to be modified or deleted.

**Self-describing messages:** All messages returned to the client to contain enough information to describe how they should handle the information.

**Hypermedia as the engine for changing application states:** after accessing a resource, the REST client must discover all the other actions available through hyperlinks. These constraints may seem difficult to enforce, but they are less so than a protocol in reality. It is for this reason that RESTful APIs are taking precedence over SOAP APIs.

In recent years, the Open API specification has established itself as the common standard for defining REST APIs. The OpenAPI standard allows developers to build REST API interfaces in a way that users can understand them with a minimum of guesswork.

## SOA and Micro Services Architectures

The two architectural approaches that use remote APIs the most are Service Oriented Architecture (SOA) and Microservices Architecture. SOA is the oldest approach. It was originally aimed at improving monolithic applications. By definition, a monolithic application does it all. However, some functions can be provided by other loosely coupled applications via an integration model, such as an ESB (Enterprise Service Bus).

While SOA is simpler than a monolithic architecture in many ways, it can potentially cause cascading changes within the environment if the interactions between the different components are not fully understood. The SOA architecture reintroduces some of the problems it sought to solve by making the environment more complex.

Microservice architectures work in a very similar way, in that they use loosely coupled services. On the other hand, they push the destructuring of classical architecture even further. The services that make up the microservices architecture use a common messaging framework, such as RESTful APIs. They use RESTful APIs to communicate with each other easily, without converting their data or resorting to additional layers of integration. RESTful APIs enable and even promote the acceleration of the distribution of new features and updates. Each service is distinct. You can replace, improve, or remove any of them without affecting the other architecture services.

**Businesses grow with APIs**

The potential of a business can be expanded when it offers an API. Having an API available, with developers willing to build on it, can extend their offerings to as many people as possible.

# How is the API of Google Calendar different from the API of all other remote servers?

In technical terms, the difference is the format of the request and the response. To render the whole page web, your browser would wait for an HTML response, which contains presentation code, while calling the Google Calendar API would return the data - probably in a format like JSON.

If your website's server is making the API request, your website's server is the client (similar to your browser being the client when you use it to access a website). From your users' perspective, APIs allow them to act without leaving your site. Most modern websites use at least some third-party APIs. Many problems already have a third-party solution, whether in the form of a library or a service. It is often easier and more reliable to use an existing solution. It is not uncommon for development teams to divide their application into several servers that talk to each other through APIs.

Servers that perform helper functions for the back-end application server are commonly referred to as microservices. In summary, when a company offers an API to its customers, it just means that it has created a set of dedicated URLs that return pure data responses, meaning the responses will not contain the type of presentation that they are. You would expect in a graphical user interface like a website. Can you make these requests with your browser? Most of the time, yes. Since the actual HTTP transmission occurs in the text, your browser will always do its best to display the response.

# CHAPTER FOUR

## BUILDING A WEB CRAWLER

---

Let's talk about this popular system design interview question-how to build a web crawler? Web crawlers are one of the most commonly used systems today. The most popular example is Google's use of crawlers to collect information from all websites. In addition to search engines, news sites also need crawlers to aggregate data sources. It seems that as long as you want to aggregate a lot of information, you can consider using crawlers.

There are many factors in building a web crawler, especially when you want to expand the system. This is why this has become one of the most popular system design interview questions. This chapter will discuss topics ranging from basic crawlers to large crawlers and discuss various interview problems.

## Basic solution

Before the system design interview, we have already talked about some important things to know before the system design interview," one of them is to start with simple things. Let's focus on building a basic web crawler that runs on a single thread. With this simple solution, we can continue to optimize.

To crawl a single web page, we only need to make an HTTP GET request to the corresponding URL and parse the response data, the crawler's core. With this in mind, a basic web crawler can work like this:

Start with the URL pool that contains all the sites we want to crawl. For each URL, issue an HTTP GET request to get the content of the web page. Parse the content (usually HTML) and extract the potential URLs we want to crawl. Add new URLs to the pool and keep crawling.

Depending on the specific problem, sometimes, we may have a separate system to generate crawl URLs.

For example, a program can continuously monitor RSS subscriptions, and for each new article, the URL can be added to the crawl pool.

## Scale issue

As we all know, any system will face a series of problems after expansion. In a web crawler, when the system is extended to multiple machines, many things can go wrong. Please take a few minutes to think about distributed web crawlers' bottleneck before jumping into details and how to solve this problem.

## Crawl frequency

**How often do you crawl the website?**

This may not sound like a big deal unless the system reaches a certain scale, and you need very fresh content. For example, if you want to get the latest news from the last hour, the crawler may need to crawl news sites every hour continuously. **But what's the problem?**

For some small websites, their servers may not be able to handle such frequent requests. One way is to follow each site robot.txt. For those who don't know robot.txt. This is the standard for communication between websites and web crawlers. It can specify what files should not be crawled, and most web crawlers follow the configuration. Besides, you can set different crawl frequencies for different websites. Usually, only a few websites need to be crawled multiple times a day.

## Deduplication

On a machine, you can keep the URL pool in memory and delete duplicate entries. However, things in distributed systems become more complicated. Multiple crawlers can extract the same URL from different web pages, and they all want to add this URL to the URL pool. Of course, it doesn't make sense to crawl the same page multiple times.

A commonly used method is to use Bloom Filter. In short, Bloom filter is a space-saving system that allows you to test whether an element is in a collection.

However, it may have false positives. In other words, if the Bloom filter can tell you that a URL is not in the pool, or possibly in the pool.

To briefly explain how the bloom filter works, the empty bloom filter is an array of mbits (full 0). There hash function, mapping each element into ma bits. So, when we add a new element (URL) to the Bloom filter, we will get the kbits from the hash function and set them all to 1.

Therefore, when we check an element's existence, we first get kBit; if any of them is not 1, we immediately know that the element does not exist. However, if all the kbits are 1, this may come from a combination of several other elements. Bloom filter is a commonly used technique, and it is a perfect solution for removing duplicate URLs in web crawlers.

## Parsing

After getting the website's response data, the next step is to parse the data (usually HTML) to extract the information we care about. This sounds like a simple thing, but it may be difficult to make it robust.

The challenge we face is that you will always find strange tags, URLs, etc. in the HTML code, and it is difficult to cover all boundary conditions. For example, when HTML contains non-Unicode characters, you may need to deal with encoding and decoding issues. Also, when the web page contains pictures, videos, or even PDF, it can cause strange behavior. Besides, some web pages are rendered with Javascript like AngularJS, and your crawler may not be able to get any content.

I would say that without a silver bullet, a perfect and robust crawler cannot be made for all web pages. You need a lot of robustness testing to make sure it works as expected.

**Conclusion**

There are many interesting topics that I haven't touched yet, but I want to mention some of them so that you can think about. One thing is to detect loops. Many websites contain links. For example, A->B->C->A, your crawler may run forever.

# CHAPTER FIVE

## CREATING A SHORT URL SYSTEM

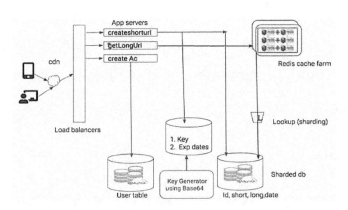

If you have started preparing for system design interviews, you must have heard of one of the most popular questions-creating a short URL system. If you are not familiar with short URLs, I will briefly explain them in this chapter. A short URL is a URL shortening service, a web service that provides short aliases to redirect long URLs. There are many other similar services, such as Google URL Shortener, Bitly, etc.

For example, URL http://blog.gainlo.co/index.php/20 15/10/22/8-things-you-need-to-know-before-system-design-interviews/ is very long and hard to remember. The short URL can create an alias for it- http://tinyurl. com/j7ve58y. If you click on the alias, it will redirect you to the original URL.

So, if you design this system to allow people to enter URLs and generate shorter alias URLs, what would you do?

**Outline**

Let's start with basic and summary solutions, and then continue to optimize. At first glance, each long URL and the corresponding alias form a key-value pair. I hope you can immediately think about things related to hashing. Therefore, the problem can be simplified this way-given a URL, how do we find a hash function that maps the URL to a short alias:

F(URL) = alias

And meet the following conditions:

Each URL can only be mapped to a unique alias. Each alias can be easily mapped back to a unique URL. The second condition is to run the actual core; the system should search through aliases and quickly redirect to the corresponding URL.

**Basic solution**

- Base64 ((A-Z) + (a-z) + (0-9) + (-) + (_). (64 Characters))
- Key generator engine
- Redis cache
- Load balancers
- MySql database

For convenience, we can assume alias http://tinyurl .com/<alias_hash>, alias_hasha string of fixed length. If the length is 7, and contains [A-Z, a-z, 0-9], you can provide $62 \wedge 7 \sim= 3500$ {Za URL.

First, we store all the mappings in a database. A simple method is to use alias_hashas, the ID of each mapping, to generate a random string of length 7.

41

So, we can store it first <ID, URL>. When the user enters a long URL http://www.gainlo.co, the system creates a random 7-character string, such abcd123as an ID, and inserts the entry <"abcd123", "http://www. gainlo.co">into the database. During operation, when someone visits http://tinyurl.com/abcd123, we abcd123 find and redirect to the corresponding URL by ID http://www. gainlo.co.

## Performance vs. flexibility

There are many follow-up questions to this question. I want to discuss here further that by using GUID (Globally Unique Identifier) as the item ID, in this question, what are the pros and cons compared to self-incrementing ID?

If you understand the insertion/query process in-depth, you will notice that using a random string as an ID may sacrifice a little performance. More specifically, when you already have millions of records, inserting can be expensive. Since the ID is not continuous, the database needs to check the ID's correct page every time a new record is inserted. However, when using incremental IDs, insertion can be easier-just going to the last page.

So, one way to optimize this is to use incremental IDs. Every time a new URL is inserted, we will add 1 to the new entry. We also need a hash function to map each integer ID to a 7-character string. If we treat each string as a 62-base number, the mapping should be easy (of course, there are other methods).

On the other hand, using incremental IDs will make the mapping more inflexible. For example, if the system allows users to set custom short URLs, the GUID solution is easier because, for any custom short URL, we can calculate the corresponding hash as the entry ID. Note: In this case, we may not use randomly generated keys, but use a better hash function to map any short URL to ID, for example, some traditional hash functions, such as CRC32, SHA-1, etc.

## Overhead

I rarely ask how to evaluate the overhead of the system. For the insert/query, we have already discussed it above. So, I will pay more attention to storage overhead.

Each entry is stored as <ID, URL>, where ID is a 7-character string. Assuming that the maximum URL length is 2083 characters, it is required for each entry $7 * 4 + 2083 * 4 = 8.4$ KB. If we store one million URL mappings, we need about 8.4G of storage space.

If we consider the database index's size, we may also store other information, such as user ID, date, etc., which requires more storage space.

## Multiple machines

When the system develops to a certain scale, a single machine cannot store all the mappings.

The more general problem is how to store hash maps on multiple machines. If you know distributed key-value storage, you should know that this can be a very complex problem.

In short, if you want to store a large number of key-value pairs in multiple instances, you need to design a search algorithm to find the corresponding machine for a given search key.

For example, if the incoming short name is http://tinyurl.com/abcd123, based on the key abcd123, the system should know which machine stores the database, and it contains the entry for this key. This is the same as database sharding.

A common method is to let the machine act as a proxy, responsible for dispatching the request to the corresponding back-end storage based on the lookup key. The back-end storage is the database that stores the mapping. They can be split in various ways, such as using hash(key) the mapping to divide into 1024 memories.

Many details can complicate the system; I just give a few examples here:

**Copy:** Data storage may crash due to various random reasons, so the common solution is to have multiple copies of each database.

**Resharding:** When the system is expanded to another level, the original fragmentation algorithm may not work properly. We may need to use a new hash algorithm to re-shard the system.

**Concurrency:** There can be multiple users inserting the same URL or editing the same alias simultaneously. With a machine, you can control it with a lock. However, when you scale to multiple instances, the situation becomes more complicated.

**Conclusion**

I think you have realized that this problem is not complicated at first glance, but when you dig into more details, especially when considering the scale issue, you will encounter many follow-up problems.

# CHAPTER SIX

## HOW TO DESIGN GOOGLE DOCS

System design interviews can be quite open and require extensive knowledge. To prepare for such an interview, it is important to cover different areas, rather than focus on a single topic. We spent a lot of time selecting system design issues for analysis. I will assume that everyone knows what Google Docs is and will not waste time introducing this product.

At first glance, this problem looks quite common, but it is true. Google Docs is a huge system with many functions. If you spend a few minutes thinking about this problem, you may realize that Google Docs is much more complicated than it seems.

As an interviewer, I don't want to limit the discussion's scope to this product's specific features. On the contrary, I tend to raise this question to know how the candidate will gradually resolve a vague question.

## Divided into components

Earlier, one way to abstract the solution is to divide the large system into smaller components. Google Docs is a huge system with a series of functions, including document storage, sharing, formatting, editing, etc. I can hardly solve such a big problem without breaking it down into different sub-problems.

If you haven't considered this question, please take 5-10 minutes to answer it yourself before reviewing our analysis. In addition, it is worth noting that if your solution is different from ours, then the problem is open, which is no problem.

We can divide the whole system into the following main parts:

**File storage:** Since Google Docs is part of Google Drive, I also include storage. The system allows users to store files (documents) into folders and support editing/creating/deleting functions. It is like an operating system.

**Online editing and formatting:** There is no doubt that one of the core functions of Google Docs is online editing. It supports almost all Microsoft Office operations, maybe more.

**Cooperation:** Google Docs allows multiple people to edit a single document simultaneously, which is amazing. This is a technical challenge.

Access control: You can share documents with your friends and give different permissions (owner, read-only, allow comments, etc.).

Some less important functions are ignored here, like plug-ins, spell checking, publishing to the web, etc.

## Storage and formatting

I put these two topics together because, in implementing storage and formatting, a very basic preliminary version of Google Docs will be created. Even without access control and collaboration, a single user can still use it to edit documents.

Besides, storage and formatting can be regarded as backend and frontend to a certain extent. IMHO, the storage system of Google Docs (or Google Drive), is very close to the operating system. It has concepts like folders, files, owners, etc.

Therefore, to build such a system, a basic building block is a file object that contains content, parent, owner, and other metadata such as creation date. The parent item represents the folder relationship, and the parent item of the root directory is empty. I will not discuss how to expand the system because building a distributed system can be very complicated. There are many things to consider, such as consistency and replication.

For the front-end formatting, an interesting question is how to store documents in the corresponding format. If you know Markdown, it is one of the best solutions. Although Google Docs may be more complicated, the basic ideas of Markdown still apply.

## Concurrent

One of the coolest features of Google Docs is the ability to edit multiple documents simultaneously. You can't just let everyone work on their own and then merge everyone's copies or pick the last edit. If you have tried the collaborative editing feature, you can see what the other party is doing and get instant feedback.

If you have used Git for version control (Translator's Note: or simply diffand patch), some of the ideas here can be similar. First, let us consider the simplest case; only two people are editing the same document. Assuming the document is ABC.

Basically, the server can keep the same number of documents for everyone and track the complete revision history. When you edit the document by adding at the beginning, this change will be sent to the server along with the last revision seen by A. Assume that B deletes the last character at this time c, and this change is also sent to the server in this way.

Since the server knows which version the modification is made on, it will adjust the changes accordingly. More specifically, B's change is to delete the third character c, and it will be converted to delete the fourth character because A was added at the beginning x.

This is the so-called Operational Transformation. It doesn't matter if you have never heard of it. The basic idea is to transform everyone's changes based on changes and other collaborators' changes.

## Access control

Google Docs allows you to invite collaborators with different levels of permissions. The naive solution shouldn't be difficult. For each file, you can maintain a list of partners with corresponding permissions, such as read-only, owner, etc. When a person wants to do a specific action, the system checks his permissions.

Usually, I would like to ask what are the challenges faced by this access control system. As we all know, there may be many problems when expanding the system to millions of users. The few things I want to mention here are:

**Speed:** When the owner updates a folder (for example, to delete a specific viewer), the update should be propagated to all its children. Speed may be an issue.

**Consistency:** When there are multiple copies, it is especially important to maintain the consistency of each copy, especially when multiple people update permissions at the same time.

Spread: There may be many cases of transmission. In addition to updating the permissions of the folder, which should be reflected in all child files, if you permit someone to read document D, then he may already have the permission to read all parent folders of document D. If someone deletes the D file, we may revoke the reading permission of D's parent folder (maybe not, this is more like a product decision).

## Conclusion

Designing a complex system like Google Docs can be scary. But once you divide the system into smaller components, it becomes much simpler.

# CHAPTER SEVEN

## DESIGNING YOUTUBE

---

Facing this problem, most people's minds are empty because they don't know where to start because this problem is too broad. Mere storage is not important, because seamlessly providing videos/images to hundreds of millions of users is very complicated. We can simplify the system into a few main components as follows:

**Storage:** How do you design the database outline? What database is used? Videos and images can be a subtopic because their storage is very special.

**Scalability:** When you have millions or even billions of users, how do you expand storage and the entire system? This may be a very complex issue, but we can at least discuss some general ideas.

**Network Server:** The most common structure is that the front-end (mobile and web) communicates with a web server. The web server handles user authentication, conversation, and logic for obtaining and updating user data. Then the server is connected to multiple backends, such as video storage, recommendation server, etc. Caching is another important component. We need multi-layer caching, like web servers, video servers, etc. There are recommendation systems, security systems, and other important components. As you can see, each feature can be used as an independent interview question.

## Storage and data model

If you are using a relational database like MySQL, then designing the data model may be simple. Youtube has used MySQL as its main database from the beginning, and it has worked very well. First, we need to define the user model, which can be stored in a table, including email, name, registration data, profile information, etc. Another common method is to save user data in two tables-one for identity verification such as email, password, name, registration date, and the other for additional personal information such as an address and age Wait.

The second main model is the video. A video contains a lot of information, including metadata (title, descrption, size, etc.), video files, comments, views, counts, etc. The basic video information should be stored in different tables so that we can have a video table. The relationship between author and video will be another table, mapping user ID to video ID. The user's favorite relationship with the video can also be a separate table. The idea here is to normalize the database-organize columns and tables to reduce data redundancy and improve data integrity.

## Video and image storage

It is recommended to store large static files (such as videos and images) separately because it has better performance and is easier to organize and expand. Youtube has more images than videos, which is very unintuitive. Imagine that each video has different size thumbnails on different screens, and the result is four times more pictures than videos. So, we should not neglect image storage.

One of the most commonly used methods is to use CDN (Content Delivery Network). In short, CDN is a globally distributed network of proxy servers deployed in multiple data centers. The goal of CDN is to provide high-availability and high-performance content to end-users. This is a third-party network, and many companies are storing static files on the CDN.

CDN's biggest advantage is that CDN can copy content in multiple places, so the content is closer to the user, there are fewer hops, and the content will run through a more friendly network. In addition, CDN is responsible for dealing with issues such as scalability, and you only need to pay for the service.

## Popular VS Long Tail Video

If you think that CDN is the ultimate solution, then you are completely wrong. Considering the number of YouTube videos today (819,417,600 hours of videos), it would be very expensive to put them all on the CDN, especially since most videos are long-tailed. These videos are only viewed 1-20 times a day.

However, one of the most interesting things about the Internet is usually the long tail content that attracts most users. The reason is simple-those popular content can be seen everywhere, and only the long tail can make the product special.

Back to the storage problem. An easy way is to host popular videos in the CDN, while less popular videos are stored in our server by location. This has two benefits:

Popular videos are watched by many viewers in different locations, which is what CDN is good at. It replicates content in multiple places so that it is more likely to provide videos from a close and friendly network. A specific group of people usually consumes Long-tail videos, and if it can be predicted in advance, these contents can be stored efficiently.

## Extended database

Once a product has millions or even billions of users, there are many problems to be solved. Scalability is one of the most important problems to be solved. Storing all data in a single database is not only inefficient but also infeasible. So how to expand Youtube's database?

When expanding the database, we can follow many general rules. The most common method is to scale on demand. In other words, it is not recommended to partition the database on the first day, because it is almost certain that when the expansion is needed, the entire infrastructure and products have undergone tremendous changes.

So, the idea started with a server. Later, you can evolve into a master and multiple read slave (master/slave model). And at some point, you will have to partition the database and adopt a sharding approach. For example, you can split the database by the user's location, and when the request arrives, route the request to the corresponding database.

For Youtube, we can further optimize it. The most important feature of YouTube is video. Therefore, we can prioritize traffic by dividing the data into two clusters: the video cluster and the general cluster. We can provide many video cluster resources, and other social network functions will be routed to the weaker cluster. The more general idea here is that you should first identify the bottleneck and optimize it when solving scalability issues. In this case, the bottleneck is watching the video

## Cache

First, when it comes to caching, most people's response is server caching. Front-end caching is equally important. If you want to make your website faster and have lower latency, you cannot avoid setting up a cache for the front end. This is a very common technique when building a website interface.

Second, as we briefly discussed in the previous article, caching does not benefit from serving video. This is mainly because most of Youtube's use cases come from these long-tail videos, and setting up a cache for all videos is expensive. So, the general idea here is that building such a long-tail product doesn't bet too much on the cache.

## Safety

There are many safe things to discuss on Youtube. I want to introduce an interesting topic here-the hacking of watching. Under each Youtube video, it shows the view count, which shows how popular the video is. People can programmatically send requests to crack the number of views, so how should we protect it?

The most straightforward way is if a particular IP makes too many requests, just block it. Or we can even limit the number of views per IP. The system can also check information such as the browser proxy and the user's history, which may prevent hacking. People can use Tor to hide IP, and sites like Mechanical Turk allow users to click on videos at a very low cost. However, hacking the system is much more difficult than most people think. For example, a video with a high number of views, but low participation is very suspicious. There are a large number of Youtube videos, and it is not difficult to extract the actual number of views. To crack the system, you need to provide a reasonable level of participation, such as the number of shares, the number of comments, the viewing time, etc. It is almost impossible to fake all of them.

## Web Server

Many people ignore the Web server because it does not have many discussions in terms of system design. But for a large system like Youtube, there are many things to consider. I want to share some of the techniques used by Youtube.

The Youtube server was originally built in Python, which allowed for fast and flexible development and deployment. You may notice that many startups choose

Python as their server language because the iteration speed is much faster. Python sometimes encounters performance problems, but many C extensions allow you to optimize key parts. This is exactly how Youtube works. To scale a web server, you can simply have multiple copies and build a load balancer on top of them. The server is mainly responsible for processing user requests and returning responses. It should have several important logics, and everything else should be built on different servers. For example, the suggestion should be an independent component for the Python server to obtain data from.

# CHAPTER EIGHT

## RATE LIMITING STRATEGIES AND METHODS

This chapter introduces the reasons for using rate limiting, the strategies and methods of rate-limiting, and under what circumstances rate limiting is related to Google Cloud products. Most of the information applies to multiple technology stack levels, but this document focuses on rate-limiting at the application level. The rate limit refers to preventing the operating frequency from exceeding certain limits. In large systems, rate limiting is usually used to protect the underlying services and resources.

## Reasons for using rate limiting

Rate limiting is usually implemented as a defensive measure for services. Shared services need to protect themselves from overuse (whether intentionally or unintentionally) to maintain service availability. Even a highly scalable system should limit usage to a certain extent. To make the system perform well, you must also consider rate-limiting when designing the client to reduce the possibility of cascading failures. Client-side and server-side rate limiting is essential to maximize throughput and minimize the end-to-end latency of large distributed systems.

## Prevent resource exhaustion

The most common reason for rate limiting is to improve the availability of API-based services by avoiding resource exhaustion. In large-scale systems, many load-based denials of service events are accidents. The cause of these events is software or configuration errors in other parts of the system, rather than malicious attacks (such as a network-based distributed denial of service attacks). Resource exhaustion that is not caused by a malicious attack is sometimes called a friendly-fire denial-of-service attack (DoS).

Usually, the service will apply rate-limiting steps before the restricted resource, and some safety margin factors will be considered. The safety margin must be considered because there may be some delays in loading, and rate-limiting . protection must be implemented before serious resource contention occurs. For example, a RESTful API may apply rate limiting to protect the underlying database; without rate limiting, a scalable API service can make a large number of calls to the database simultaneously. The database may not be able to send a clear rate limiting signal.

## Manage policies and quotas

If the service capacity is shared among multiple users or users, rate limiting can be applied to each user to provide reasonable usage without affecting other users. These limits may apply to longer periods, or they may apply to resources that are not measured by rate but measured by the amount allocated. These rates and allocation limits are collectively referred to as quotas. Quotas can also be applied to API monetization packages or free tier restrictions.

It's important to understand how the apps and projects in your organization share these quotas. For example, an out-of-control Canary version in a production project may consume quotas of resources used by the production service infrastructure.

## Control flow

In complex, correlated systems that process large amounts of data and messages, you can use rate-limiting to control these flows-whether you are merging multiple data flows into a single service or distributing a single work data flow to multiple workers.

For example, you can distribute work more evenly among workers by restricting the flow to each worker, thereby preventing a single worker from accumulating a queue of unprocessed items when other workers are idle. Flow control must prepare the pre-fetched data for processing locally and ensure that each node in the system has an equal opportunity to complete the work. For details, see the Pub/Sub: Flow Control section.

## Avoid overcharge

You can use rate-limiting to control costs, for example, if the underlying resource can automatically scale to meet demand, but the budget for that resource is limited. Organizations may use rate-limiting to prevent experimentation from getting out of control and to increase free use. Part of the reason for this concern is why many Google Cloud quotas have initial values that can be increased upon request. Organizations that provide fixed-fee SaaS (software as a service) solutions may apply other fee-driven rate limits to establish a fee, price, and profit models for each customer.

## Strategy

In the service chain or grid, many nodes of the system are clients and servers. Each part of the system may not have any rate-limiting strategy applied, or one or more strategies may be combined in different ways, so you need to look at the entire system to make sure every-thing is running in the best way. Even when rate limiting is fully implemented on the server-side, the client should be designed to respond appropriately.

In most cases, if the tools or infrastructure used to implement rate limiting strategies fail or become inaccessible, your service should activate the "emergency start" function and try to handle all requests. The client usually does not exceed the quota, and the "emergency turn on" function is less destructive to large-scale systems than the "emergency turn off" function.

The "emergency shutdown" function will cause complete interruption, while the "emergency opening" function will only cause performance degradation. Decisions about "emergency turn on" or "emergency turn off" are mainly related to the server-side, but knowing what retry method the client uses to determine whether the request has failed may affect your decision on server behavior.

# No rate limits

Be sure to consider not implementing rate-limiting as the basis for the design, which is the worst case the system must adapt to. Implement reliable error handling mechanisms when building your system if some of your rate limiting strategies fail, and understand what your service users will receive in these situations. Be sure to provide useful error codes and ensure that no sensitive data is leaked in the error codes. Using timeouts, deadlines, and fusing modes can help improve service reliability without rate limiting.

If your service calls other services to complete the request, you can choose how to pass any restriction signals from these services back to the original caller.

Note: In the HTTP service, the service showed that the most common way they are applied is rate-limiting in 429 return HTTP response status code. The response can provide additional details to explain the reason for the application restriction (for example, the quota for freemium users is low, or the system is under maintenance).

The simplest solution is to only forward rate-limiting responses from downstream services to the caller. Another option is to enforce rate limits on behalf of downstream services and block callers.

## Enforce rate limit

The most common rate-limiting strategy is to let the service apply one or more ways to enforce rate limiting. This rate limit may be implemented to protect the service directly or protect downstream resources if the downstream service cannot protect itself. For example, suppose you are running an API service to connect to a legacy backend system that is not resilient under high load. In that case, the API service should not use a pass-through strategy (assuming that the legacy service will provide its rate-limiting signal).

If you need to enforce a rate limit, first understand why the rate limit is applied in this situation, and then determine which characteristics of the request are most suitable for use as a limit key (source IP address, user, and API key). After you select the restriction key, the implemented restriction can use it to track usage. When the limit is reached, the service returns a limit signal (usually a 429HTTP response).

## Delayed response

If computing the response is expensive or time-consuming, the system may not provide a fast response to the request, making it difficult for the service to handle high-frequency requests. In these cases, an alternative to rate limiting is to offload the request to a queue and return some form of job ID. This allows the service to maintain higher availability and reduces the computational workload that the client may block the call for a long time while waiting for a response. How the delayed response result is returned to the caller is another set of choices. It usually involves polling the job ID status or polling the event-based system where the caller can register for callbacks or subscribe to event channels. Such systems are beyond the scope of this document.

If the request's immediate response does not contain any actual information, the delayed response mode is the easiest to apply. If this mode is overused, it may increase system complexity and failure modes.

## Client policy

The strategies introduced so far apply to server-side rate limiting. However, these strategies can provide references for client design, especially considering that many distributed system components are both clients and servers.

Just as the main purpose of service usage rate limiting is to protect itself and maintain availability, the client's main purpose is to complete sending requests to the service. The service may not be able to complete the request from the client due to various reasons, including the following:

1. The service cannot be accessed due to network conditions.

2. The service returned an unknown error.

3. The service rejected the request due to a failed authentication or authorization.

4. The client's request is invalid or malformed.

5. Services will limit the caller's rate and send back a pressure signal (usually a 429response).

We recommend that you design the client to be flexible in dealing with these types of problems. The client library provided by Google has many built-in functions to recognize the above scenarios.

Clients should generally retry the request after a delay to respond to rate limits, interruptions, or unknown errors. The best practice is to increase this delay exponentially after each failed request (called exponential backoff). If many clients may issue schedule-based requests (such as fetching results every hour), additional random time (jitter) To request time and off period to ensure that the plurality of client instance will not cause periodic shock group effect (thundering herd), but does not itself produce some form of DDoS.

Imagine that a mobile application with many users happens to check-in via the API at noon every day and apply the same deterministic backoff logic. Many clients will call the service at noon, which will start to rate limit and return the status code for the 429response. The client will then dutifully back off and just wait for the set time (deterministic delay) 60 seconds, and then at 12:01, the service will receive another large request set. By adding a random offset (jitter) to the initial request time or delay time, requests and retries can be distributed more evenly, giving the service a better chance to complete the request.

Ideally, non-idempotent requests can be issued in the context of a strongly consistent transaction. Still, not all service requests can provide such guarantees, so retrying these changed data needs to consider the consequences of repeated operations.

Suppose the client developer knows that the called system cannot flexibly cope with the pressure load and does not support the rate limit signal (back pressure). In that case, the client library developer or client application developer can pass the enforcement that can be used on the server-side. The method of rate limiting is to choose to apply the limit yourself.

Suppose the API client uses an asynchronous long-running operation ID to delay the response. In that case, the client can choose to enter a locked loop to poll for the delayed response state, thereby eliminating this complexity for the client library users.

## Ways to enforce rate limits

Generally speaking, the rate is a simple count of the number of occurrences of an instance over time. However, there are several different ways of measuring and limiting rates, each of which has its purpose and impact.

**Token bucket:** The token bucket maintains a rolling and accumulated usage budget to balance tokens. This method can identify that not all inputs of the service correspond to the request one-to-one. The token bucket adds tokens at a certain rate. When a service request is issued, the service will try to revoke the token (reduce the number of tokens) to complete the request. If there are no tokens in the token bucket, the service has reached its limit and returns a back pressure response. For example, in a GraphQL service, a single request may cause multiple operations to be combined into one result. These operations may each obtain a token. In this way, the service can track the capacity to limit its usage instead of directly associating the rate-limiting method with the request.

**Leaky bucket:** The leaky bucket is similar to the token bucket, but the bucket's number of leaks limits the rate. This method can recognize that the system will provide a certain degree of limited capacity to save the request before the service can process it; any additional content just overflows the edge and is discarded. This buffer capacity (but not necessarily using leaky buckets) also applies to components near the service, such as load balancers and disk I/O buffers.

**Fixed period:** Fixed time period limits (such as 3000 requests per hour or ten requests per day) are easy to declare, but due to the reset of the available quota, these limits will be limited by peaks that occur at the edge of the time period. For example, imagine a limit of 3000 requests per hour, which still allows all 3000 requests (peak) to be issued in the first minute of the hour, and the service may be overloaded as a result.

**Sliding period:** Sliding period has the advantage of a fixed period, but the rolling period can eliminate unexpected problems. Systems such as Redis using expired keys to assist this approach.

Suppose you have many independently running service instances (such as Cloud Functions) in a distributed system, and the service needs to be restricted as a whole. In that case, you need to use a logical global (global for all running functions, not necessarily geographical the global) quick key-value pair storage area (such as Redis) to synchronize various limit counters.

## Rate limiting feature in Google Cloud

Each Google API (internal and external) enforces a certain level of rate limits or quotas. This is the basic principle of Google service design. This section explains how these services also expose rate-limiting as a feature you can use when building on Google Cloud.

## Quota and cap

Google Cloud enforces quotas to limit the amount of specific Google Cloud resources that your project can use. Rate quota Specify the number of resources that can be used at a given time, such as the number of API requests per day. You can also set your limits on the number of resources that can be used at a given time; such custom limits are called "caps."

Each Google Cloud product has a page that lists service limits (for example, the maximum message size) and rate-based quotas (for example, the maximum number of queries per second for a specific API). These pages will also indicate whether you can apply to increase your quota. To find these pages, start this search.

Generally, Google Cloud quotas are calculated on a project basis, and time periods are calculated on a second or minute basis. If multiple parts of your solution are running in a project, it is important to note that they share these quotas.

You can monitor quotas' consumption and even set reminders to remind you that quota usage has changed or usage exceeds a certain amount. You can set your upper limit for API usage and use budget reminders to control API usage costs.

## Cloud Tasks

Cloud Tasks is a fully managed service that can manage the execution, scheduling, and delivery of many distributed tasks. With Cloud Tasks, you can perform work asynchronously in addition to user requests. Cloud Tasks allows you to set rate and concurrency limits at the same time. Cloud Tasks use the token bucket method to achieve a certain degree of burstiness in delivering messages within these limits.

## Cloud Functions

Cloud Functions is a lightweight computing solution that allows developers to create single-purpose independent functions that can respond to cloud events without managing servers or runtime environments. By default, Cloud Functions are stateless and highly scalable.

Google's managed infrastructure automatically creates function instances to handle incoming request load. Due to this scaling behavior, functions may become the target of high-frequency requests, and if these functions call downstream services, it may cause unexpected DoS on these downstream services.

One type of DoS is the exhaustion of database connections. Suppose each function instance establishes a database connection to the backend. In that case, the traffic peak may cause multiple instances to be automatically expanded vertically, and the available connection capacity on the database server will be exhausted. To prevent the function from expanding beyond a certain number of instances, the service provides an upper limit set for each function's number of instances.

For background functions, Google Cloud uses the event payload and context to call your function. You can specify that you want the system to retry event delivery when it fails or cannot process it (perhaps because of a downstream resource rate-limit the event).

Although the upper limit setting of the number of instances can help you limit the concurrency setting, you cannot directly control the number of times your function can be called per second through the upper limit setting. Please refer to the Next Steps section to find a tutorial that demonstrates how to use Redis to coordinate rate limiting across functions globally.

## Pub/Sub: flow control

Pub/Sub is a fully-managed real-time messaging service that allows you to send and receive messages between independent applications. When moving a large number of messages through Pub/Sub topics, you may need to adjust the message processing rate in the consuming client to ensure that concurrent users are effective and do not retain too many outstanding messages so that the overall processing delay is not affected. To adjust this behavior, Pub/Sub clients need to expose multiple flow control settings.

## Cloud Run

Cloud Run is a managed computing platform for you to run stateless containers invoked via HTTP requests.

Unlike Cloud Functions, if the service stack in the container supports it, a single container instance can process multiple requests concurrently.

## Istio

Istio is an open-source independent service grid that can provide you with the foundation you need to run a distributed microservice architecture successfully. Elastic microservices architecture requires services to defend against malicious peer-to-peer services, so Istio directly provides rate limiting in the service mesh.

## Cloud Endpoints

Cloud Endpoints is an API management system that helps you protect, monitor, and analyze APIs and set API quotas using the same infrastructure that Google uses for its APIs. This service is designed to help you expose your service to external users, allowing you to configure your quota (including rate-based policies).

## Apigee

Apigee Edge is a platform for developing and managing API agents. The API proxy provides an interface for developers who want to use your back-end services. Developers do not use these services directly, but instead, access the Edge API proxy created by you. It is common to put Apigee in front of backend services that may not have its rate-limiting feature, so rate limiting is a built-in feature of Apigee Edge.

## Google Cloud Armor

Google Cloud Armor uses Google's global infrastructure and security systems to defend against distributed denial of service (DDoS) attacks against infrastructure and applications. This includes built-in logic regarding malicious spikes and high-rate loads for protected services.

## Project Shield

Although Project Shield is not a Google Cloud service, it uses Google infrastructure to protect eligible websites from DDoS attacks.

## Other ways to increase flexibility

Application-level rate limiting can provide enhanced elasticity for services, but by combining application-level rate-limiting with other methods, elasticity can be further improved.

**Caching:** Storing slower calculations results allows the service to handle higher frequency requests so that rate-limiting back pressure is not frequently applied to the client.

**Fuse:** You can temporarily lock some parts of the system latch to a silent state so that the service network can more flexibly deal with problems caused by the propagation of frequently occurring errors. For implementation examples, see the documentation Istio fuse part.

**Priority:** Not all users of the system have the same priority. When designing rate-limiting keys, please consider other factors to ensure that clients with higher priority will be served. You can use load shedding to remove the burden of lower priority traffic in the system.

**Limiting rates at multiple layers:** If your machine's network interface or operating system kernel is overwhelmed, the application layer rate-limiting feature may not have a chance to start working at all. You can apply rate-limiting on layer 3 of iptables, or local devices can limit on layer 4. The system I/O (such as disks and network buffers) applies adjustable-rate limits, and you may also be affected by these limits.

**Monitoring:** The operating system and personnel need to notice that the restriction function is working. Monitoring over-quota rates is essential for incident management and capturing software decline. We recommend implementing such monitoring from the perspective of the client and the server of the service. Not as long as a rate limit occurs, there should be a reminder that requires immediate attention from operations staff. In non-extreme situations, you can respond to the rate limit signal later as part of the system's routine evaluation and maintenance. You can use the logs about when the rate limit is applied as a signal that you need to make changes, such as increasing component capacity, requesting an increase in quota, or modifying a policy.

# CHAPTER NINE

## CREATING PHOTO SHARING APP

More specifically, the system allows people to follow each other, share/comment/ like pictures, and maybe some other functions such as exploration, advertising, etc. We want to analyze this problem here for several reasons. First, picture-sharing systems are very popular. I did not choose a strange question, which has almost no application in the real world. On the contrary, there are many similar products like Pinterest and Flickr.

Second, the question is universal, which is very common in system design interviews. Usually, the interviewer will not ask you to solve a clear problem, making many people uncomfortable. Finally, the analysis covers a wide range of scalability, databases, data analysis, etc. It can be reused in other system design interview questions.

This method's advantage is that you can know what problem you want to solve, and the interviewer is less likely to be confused. It is quite straightforward to design a picture sharing system to determine two main objects-user objects and picture objects.

I want to use a relational database to explain because it is usually easier to understand. In this case, we will have a user table containing information such as name, email, registration date, etc. The picture table is the same. In addition, we also need to store two relationships-user follow relationship and user picture relationship. This is very natural, and it is worth noting that user attention is not bidirectional. Therefore, having such a data model allows users to pay attention to each other. To check the user's information flow, we can extract all the photos from the people he follows.

**Potential scale issues**

The above solution should work fine. As an interviewer, I always want to ask when we have millions of users, how can we solve this problem?

This question is a good way to test whether the candidate can foresee potential scale problems, rather than just asking you how to solve a certain problem.

Of course, there is no standard answer; I want to list a few ideas as inspiration.

## 1. Response time

When the user reaches a certain number, it is common to see slow response time as a bottleneck.

For example, an expensive operation is to present the user's information flow. The server must check everyone that the user follows, get all the pictures from them, and rank them according to a specific algorithm. When users follow people with a large number of pictures, the operation may be slow.

Various methods can be applied here. If it is a bottle-neck, we can upgrade the ranking algorithm. If sorted by date, we can use the infinite scroll function to read the first N's most recent pictures from everyone. Or we can use an offline pipeline to pre-calculate some signals that can speed up the ranking.

The point is, someone can't follow hundreds of users, but someone may have thousands of pictures. So, the core is to speed up the acquisition and ranking of pictures.

## 2. Schema extension

When there are only dozens of users and pictures, we can store and provide everything from one server.

However, for millions of users, a single server is far from enough, due to storage, memory, and CPU limitations. This is why it is common to see server crashes when there are a large number of requests. To extend the architecture, the rule of thumb is that service-oriented architecture (SOA) is better than a single application.

Don't put everything together; it's best to divide the entire system into small components by service and separate each component. For example, we can separate the database and the load balancer (on different servers).

**3. Database extension**

Even if we put the database on a separate server, it cannot store unlimited data. At some point, we need to expand the database. For this specific problem, we can split the database into sub-databases such as the user database and comment database for vertical partitioning (Partition), or split according to attributes such as American users and European users for horizontal partitioning (Sharding).

## Information flow ranking

It is also interesting to discuss how to rank information streams (pictures) in the user's timeline. Although it is fairly simple to arrange everything in chronological order, is this the best approach? Such open-ended questions are very common in system design interviews.

There are many choices. For example, an algorithm that combines time and the user's likelihood of liking this photo is promising.

A common strategy is to propose a scoring mechanism that uses various features as indicators and calculates each picture's final score to design such an algorithm.

Intuitively, important features include the number of likes/comments, whether the user likes the owner of many photos, etc. Because of its simplicity, a linear combination can be used as a starting point. Then, it is worth trying more advanced machine learning algorithms like collaborative filtering.

## Image optimization

First, it is usually recommended to store all photos separately in production. Amazon S3 is one of the most popular storage systems. However, you don't need to be able to bring up this.

The point is that images are usually large and rarely updated. So, the independent image storage system has many advantages. For example, when the file is static, caching and copying can be much simpler.

Second, to save space, images should be compressed. A common method is to store/provide only compressed versions of images. Google Photos uses this method and provides unlimited free storage.

**Conclusion**

Also, for reference, you can check Instagram's infrastructure and Flickr architecture. However, I don't think they are very helpful for system design interviews because they are too focused on technology rather than design principles.

# CHAPTER TEN

## DESIGNING A NEWS FEED SYSTEM

Whether you are making Twitter, Instagram, or Facebook, you need some kind of news feed system to show updates from followers/friends. There are some interesting details about news feeds, such as how to sort them and optimize the release.

For simplicity, let's focus on designing Facebook's news feed system because different products have different requirements. To briefly summarize this feature, when users enter their homepage, they will see their friends' updates in a specific order. The push can contain pictures, videos, or texts, and the user may have many friends. We said before that when faced with such a large and vague system design problem, it is best to decompose the big problem into sub-problems and add some general ideas.

For the news push system, we can divide it into front-end and back-end. I will skip the front end because this is not common in system design interviews. For the backend, three sub-problems seem critical to me:

**Data model:** We need some models to store users and push objects. More importantly, when we try to optimize the system's read/write, there are many trade-offs.

**Push ranking:** Facebook's ranking is not only in chronological order.

Push release: When there are only a few hundred users, the release may be trivial. However, if there are millions or even billions of users, this may be expensive. So there is a question of scale.

**Data model**

There are two basic objects, users and tweets. For user objects, we can store user ID, name, registration date, etc. For tweet objects, there are tweet IDs, tweet types, content, metadata, etc. They should also support pictures and videos.

If we use a relational database, we also need to establish two relationships: user-tweet relationship and friend relationship. The former is very simple. We can create a user-tweet table to store the user ID and corresponding tweet ID. For a single user, if he has posted multiple tweets, it can contain multiple entries.

For friend relations, the adjacency list is one of the most common methods. If we regard all users as nodes in a giant graph, the edges connecting the nodes represent friend relationships. We can use the friend table to model the edge (friend relationship), each containing two user IDs. By doing this, most of the operations are very convenient, such as obtaining all user friends and checking whether two people are friends.

In the above design, let us see what happens when we get pushes from all user friends. The system will first obtain the user IDs of all friends from the friend's table.

Then extract the entire tweet IDs for each friend from the tweet table. Finally, extract the tweet content according to the tweet ID in the tweet table. You can see that we need to perform three connections, which will affect performance.

A common optimization is to store the tweet content and the tweet ID together in the user-tweet so that we don't need to link the tweet. This method is called denormalization, which means that we can optimize read performance (reduce the number of connections).

**Note:** There are a few problems here. Since each tweet has only one author, the author ID can be put into the tweet table without redundancy.

The disadvantages are obvious:

**Data redundancy:** We are storing redundant data, occupying storage space (classic space-time relationship).

**Data consistency:** Whenever we update a tweet, we need to update the tweet table and the user-tweet table.

Otherwise, the data is inconsistent. This increases the complexity of the system.

Remember, no one method is always better than others (normalization and denormalization).

## Rank

The most straightforward way to arrange tweets is by creation time. Obviously, Facebook does more than that. "Important" tweets are at the top. Before jumping to the ranking algorithm, I usually ask why the ranking has changed? How do we evaluate whether the new ranking algorithm is better? If the candidates raise these questions themselves, it is impressive.

The reason for optimizing ranking is not that it seems right. On the contrary, everything should happen for a reason. Suppose there are several core indicators we care about, such as user stickiness, retention rate, advertising revenue, etc. A better ranking system can significantly improve these indicators, which also answers how to assess whether progress has been made.

So back to the question, how should we rank tweets? A common strategy is to calculate tweet scores based on various characteristics and rank tweets based on the scores. This is one of the most commonly used methods for all ranking problems.

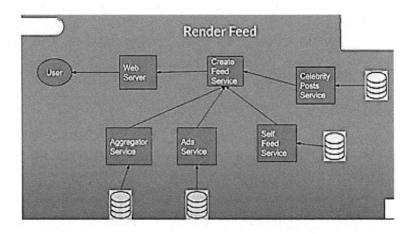

More specifically, we can select several features that are most relevant to the importance of tweets, for example, the number of shares/likes/comments, the time of update, whether the tweets have images/videos, etc. Then, the score can be calculated from these features, possibly a linear combination. For a simple ranking system, this is usually sufficient.

The overall idea of ranking is to select the relevant features/signals, and then figure out how to combine them to calculate the final score. This method is very common in many real systems. As you can see, the important things here are two things-features and calculation algorithms. To better understand it, I would like to introduce how rankings on Facebook actually work-EdgeRank briefly.

For each news update, when other users interact with the tweet, they create something that Facebook calls "edge," which includes actions such as likes and comments.

First, let's take a look at which features are used to evaluate the importance of updates/push. The ranking of edges basically uses three signals: intimacy, edge weight, and time decay.

$$\sum = \text{👪} \times \text{⚖} \times \text{⧗}$$

**Rank**          **Affinity**          **Weight**          **Decay**

**Intimacy or Affinity(u):** For each news feed, intimacy will evaluate the distance between you and this user. For example, you are more likely to care about your close friends' posts than the people you just met.

**Edge weight (e):** The edge weight basically reflects the importance of each edge. For example, comments are more important than likes.

**Time decay (d):** The older the story, the fewer users dislike it.

So how does Facebook rank based on these three characteristics? The calculation algorithm is very simple. For each tweet, you create, multiply these factors for each edge, and then add the edge scores to get the updated EdgeRank. And the higher it is, the more likely your update will appear in user pushes.

## Intimacy

We can do the same thing to assess intimacy. Various factors can be used to reflect the distance between two people. First of all, explicit interactions like comments, tags, sharing, clicks, etc. are powerful signals that we should use. Obviously, each type of interaction should have different weights. For example, there should be more comments than likes.

Second, the time factor must be tracked. Maybe you have had many exchanges with a good friend, but these are still relatively rare recently. In this case, we should reduce intimacy. So for every interaction, we should also consider the time decay factor.

## Push release

When the user loads all the pushes from his friends, this can be an expensive behavior. Keep in mind that users may have thousands of friends, and each of them can post a large number of updates, especially for high-end users. To load all tweets from friends, the system needs at least two connections (get a friend list and tweet list). So how to optimize and expand the push release system? There are basically two common ways- push and pull.

Once a user publishes a tweet for the push method, we immediately push this tweet (actually a pointer to the tweet) to all his friends. The advantage is that when extracting tweets, there is no need to browse the friend list and get the tweets from each friend. It significantly reduces read operations. However, the shortcomings are also obvious. It adds write operations, especially for people with a large number of friends.

For the pull method, tweets will only be fetched when the user is loading their homepage. Therefore, the tweet data does not need to be sent immediately after creation. You can see that this method optimizes the write operation, but even after using denormalization, obtaining data may be slow (if you don't understand it, please check our previous article). Both methods work well in certain situations, and it is best to understand their advantages and disadvantages.

**Selective fanout (fanout)**

The process of pushing events to all friends or fans is called fan-out. Therefore, the push method is also called fan-out while writing, and the pull-in method is fan-out while loading. The interviewer is more likely to ask you this question; if you have any further methods to optimize the fan-out process?

You can combine the two. Specifically, if you mainly use the push method, you can disable fan-out for advanced users, while others can only load updates during reading. The idea is that push operations can be expensive for advanced users because they have to notify many friends. By disabling their fan-out, we can save a lot of resources. Twitter has greatly improved after adopting this method.

For the same reason, once a user posts a tweet, we can limit the fan out to his active friends. For inactive users, most of the time, push operation is a waste because they will never come back to use push.

**Conclusion**

If the 80-20 rule is followed, 80% of the cost comes from 20% of the features/users. Therefore, optimization does involve the determination of bottlenecks. In addition, the push system is a very popular topic because it is now widely used by so many products.

# FINAL THOUGHT ON SYSTEM DESIGN INTERVIEW

Q: For the interview, do I need to know all the knowledge points here?

Answer: No, if you are just preparing for the interview, you don't need to know all the knowledge points.

What you will be asked in an interview depends on the following factors:

1. Your experience

2. Your technical background

3. The position you interviewed for

Those experienced candidates are usually expected to learn more about system design. Architects or team leaders are expected to learn more in addition to personal contributions. Top technology companies usually also have one or more system design interviews.

The interview will be very broad and in-depth in several areas. This will help you understand some different topics about system design. Based on your timeline, experience, interview position, and Interview Company, make appropriate adjustments to the following guidance.

Short-term-aim at the breadth of system design topics. Practice by solving some interview questions.

Mid-term-aim at the breadth and primary depth of system design topics. Practice by solving many interview questions.

Long-term aiming at the breadth and advanced depth of system design topics. Practice by solving most interview questions.

# About Author

***Maurice Jayson*** is a prolific UX and System designer who has worked for more than 12 years of his career as a UX and System designer. He understands UX and system design so perfectly that he has many online for where he teaches UX and system design. Maurice is happily married with two children.

## About the book

This system design interview book is an amazing product from Maurice Jayson. It is a systematic guide on how to answer difficult questions from System Design interviewers. Maurice has headed several panels of interviewers looking to recruit system and User interface designers and has compiled a list of recurrent question and hidden intricacy that all system designers should know when job hunting.

ISBN 9798693765177

90000

9 798693 765177